GWYRIAD

Nigel Jarrett is a Welsh writer, a former daily-newspaperman, and a double prizewinner. He won the Rhys Davies award for short fiction and the inaugural Templar Shorts award. His first collection of stories, *Funderland*, was published by Parthian and warmly reviewed in the *Independent*, the *Guardian*, and the *Times*. Parthian also published his first poetry collection, *Miners At The Quarry Pool*, described by Patricia McCarthy, editor of *Agenda*, as 'a virtuoso performance'. His second full story collection, *Who Killed Emil Kreisler?*, was published by Cultured Llama in 2016; GG Books brought out his first novel, *Slowly Burning*, in the same year. Three years later, Templar published his story pamphlet, *A Gloucester Trilogy*, and in 2022 his fictional memoir, *Notes From the Superhorse Stable*, appeared from Saron Publishers and his fourth story collection, *Five Go to Switzerland*, from Cockatrice Books. Jarrett is a regular contributor to *Jazz Journal*, *Acumen* poetry magazine, *Nation.Cymru*, the *Wales Arts Review*, and other publications. He is included in *Story*, the Library of Wales's two-volume anthology of 20th- and 21st-century Welsh short fiction. He was for many years chief music critic of the *South Wales Argus* daily newspaper.

GWYRIAD
POEMS

NIGEL JARRETT

Cockatrice Books
Y diawl a'm llaw chwith

Copyright © Nigel Jarrett 2024

First published in 2024 by Cockatrice Books

Editor: Rob Mimpriss
www.cockatrice-books.com
mail@cockatrice-books.com

The right of Nigel Jarrett to be identified as the author of the work has been asserted by him in accordance with the Copyright, Designs and Patents Act 1988.

All rights reserved. No part of this publication may be reproduced, stored in a retrieval system or transmitted in any form or by any means, electronic, mechanical, photocopying, recording or otherwise, without prior permission of the author.

Cover: Alice Kate, a servant, admitted to the Bristol Lunatic Asylum, Blackberry Hill, Fishponds, in 1894. Photograph courtesy of the Glenside Museum (formerly the Asylum church) and the Bristol Archives (ref: 40513/Med/C/CB/4/8)

CONTENTS

Another Place	11
Gulls	12
Decline	13
Hergest Ridge	15
The Mirabelle Restaurant	16
After Hemingway	17
Maps	18
Parish Newsletter	19
Observer	20
The Elché Gardens	22
Infanta at her Achilleion	23
Transporter Bridge	24
Circus Hungarica	25
When UR A Poet	26
Roll Up, Roll Up...	27
Y Fenni/Fishponds	29
Diagnosis	30
The Lunatic Act	31
Day Book	33
Sailing from Delirium	34
Would You Believe?	36
Catatonia	37
Little Mal, a Welshman	38
Janus	42
Terminus 1	43
Terminus 2	44
Notes & Observations	45
Kingfishers In Puzzle Wood	47
Patient Record: the Photograph	48
The One Light...	49
The Place	50
Answerphone	51

Muybridge's Runner	52
Wildlife	53
Collecting Folk Songs	54
Austerity	55
Schumann's Remedy	56
Marion Morehouse	58
Kirkham	59
Kempsey Murals	60
Sam. Johnson in Uttoxeter	61
Bodoni Bold	62
Fleeing the Sight of Blood and Other Departures	63
Spinsters	70
Galatea	72
Mobile Snax	73
Midwifery	74
Saddo	75
Promises	76
Cold Comfort	77
Art	78
The Wilmcote Plesiosaur	79
Persephone	80
Orchard	81
Gold Watch Scenario	82
Gland	83
Dying Now	84
Sylvia's Eleventh Hour	85
Pet	86
Pale Namibian Roses	87
A Memory Seat at St. Ives	88
No Upper Chain	90
Here Lie Loved Ones	91
Guillotine	93
Kicking Leaves	94
Symbol	95
At the Crem	96
Care Home	97
The Running of the Deer	99
Alzheimer's Castle	100

Ward C4 West	101
Notes	102
Acknowledgements	104

And does it not seem hard to you,
When all the sky is clear and blue
And I should like so much to play
To have to go to bed by day?
  From *Bed In Summer*, by Robert Louis Stevenson

It's A Mad Mad Mad Mad World
  US comedy film (United Artists 1963) directed
        by Stanley Kramer

Another Place

They could be Gormley's men, rusting
on Crosby beach for all the world
a memorial to the stragglers of Dunkirk,
or myth creatures scorched for ever; well,
Fate warned them they would be
if there was so much as a glance at Helios
during the rare collision of Mars and Saturn.

But these are yours or mine, plunged
in river-rush and alert to evasive trout.

There's no tide here: bushed at the end
of its climb upstream, it's given way
to the old route of ice melt, field cataracts,
summer's shallow roll of grit and silt.

As the fish lash to reach them, protesting,
they stand accused: wife-beaters and thieves
fled from hostility, deaf to good advice.

Gulls

They're there again, troubling
    the tip for answers, as if
a midden could illuminate
    a mob in penitential garb.
First they funnel the latest
    from the summit, then cluster
on the raked-over slopes
    of heresy and superstition.

In the vales they fare no better.
    Spirited in squalls from flint
chipped by the plough, they surf
    the furrow's wave, anticipating
their element, that skim above
    the gulf between alpha and
omega, twin mysteries ever
    in want of fluttering attention.

Decline

No retrieving of paradise here,
    which was what they called it
when we moved in with the others,
    all unused to newness, the smell
of paint just dried, the footbridge
    taking our kids to school through
trees that came with root balls, shifted
    as you'd roll a poolside umbrella,
and above the traffic, with no madmen
    to turn the little 'uns into rag dolls.

But even before his furniture arrived,
    Pritchard struck a match on the window
to light a celebratory fag, leaving a mark,
    a sulphurous etched blemish his wife
pointed to whenever he fell short,
    which he did that night Maria asked
if he could fix her flickering iron —
    a repair that involved sliding his hand
towards a strangeness awaiting him,
    a difference of structure, of possibility.

What stopped it working was the thought
    that the new was not to be defiled,
and the tendency of Maria and Jake
    to flit by moonlight rather than pay rent,
the scored arc as their fridge took
    the corner still there twenty years on;
it's always movement that corrupts
    the stasis of perfection, silent Ted's
departure included: they found him hanging
    from a tree, like a thief left out to swing.

There's been a murder at No. 7;
    at 15 they've filled the garden
with a bouncy castle snapped up on eBay,
    its Great Towers tending to deflate
and flop into 16's lettuce, 17's dahlias;
    the bridge's concrete cancer is terminal
and the trees refuse to come out.
    There are no takers for the garages
with skewed doors, or the monks huddled inside.
    Toddlers present needles, quizzically.

Hergest Ridge

(In Memoriam Francis Kilvert)

The heaving Malverns
are doubled in your eyes
here near Stanner Rocks,
where the Devil lounged in Summer
for you to flick back
the counterpane fields and ponder
all base scuttling drugged for a term
by the wisped sleep of Arcady.

The Mirabelle Restaurant

More a posh café really:
sticky flapjacks, tea leaves infusing.
Is this anyone's seat?
She says it might have been
if hubbie had not keeled over
with a stroke two years before.
She'd met a fella at Modern Ballroom.
but he'd gone too: cancer
(she tweaked a flame with thumb and finger).

She left soon after, her legacy
three tight balls of foil,
a lipstick-kissed mug and
an empty space that exhaled:
See my grief sail on the Winter wind.

It had left her raw; but now,
to the snap of a Kit-Kat,
I see it settle on intent jeweller,
old man with dog,
hoodie begging.

After Hemingway

(*To be read in an American accent*)

On a shooting trip to Bal-Mawr, we came across a vixen;
her head was caught in a snare — the neck pulled and stretched till
    no wider than a Swiss Roll.

She was frozen with pain in the heat, like some creature
whose knack of faking death to avoid the attention of dull raptors
    had been urged to boldness.

Ill-considered in her case; only the manic glazed eye moved,
twitching with what looked for all the world like embarrassment,
    or vulpine equivalent of same.

We jammed a stick between the cheese-wire and her flesh,
managing to slip the noose knot enough for her to reverse out
    and, panting, stand back as if

about to run at the loop again. Then — there's no other way
of describing it — she thought, 'To hell with that; let's make
    for home.' And she did.

A mite unsteadily, to be sure, she thithered away, her brush
drooping to cover her tracks. After twenty yards, she pulled up
    short on the ridge, a fox statue.

We didn't stay to watch but gave her an hour, wishing
we'd had the guts to pop her skull with shot when she was in
    culling position, presenting herself.

Maps

He left the high country, knowing with head bowed
that all had been contoured beyond forgiveness.
He walked the northings, crossed others going east
past pinpointed brooks where compasses had tyrannised
the innocent peak of Radnor.

And so he came to you in your square of light
at The Whittern; not that close for fear of too intimate
an acquaintance with your decline, but near enough to observe
that you, too, were marked by a convoluted wandering
and the impressive rubble of your own terminal moraine.

That tear dashed on your cheek like a phial of elixir
was to him a wild blundering beyond
The Extent Of Available Information.
You had loved those bleached spaces where things known
were denied until pale cartographers speared

the tombs of Roman widows and made of mourning a spectacle.
For you had taken bearings ahead of the fields of phantoms;
you had heard the beating hooves on the night air
above the fairy ring of Kington's high moonlit racecourse,
earth shadow of a thundering in the sun.

Parish Newsletter

We mock St Basil's next door,
when we aren't fuming or indifferent,

because we are experts on details
of its comic reversal of decline:

Norman tower, holding out against
an emblazon of Victorian improvement,

including dormer windows (a vocal trio
or the house of God domesticated?)

and woodcarver in stovepipe and stained glass,
who varnished his screen to make it last.

Once on Sundays we hear from
the random dozen of our congregation

(the magazine graphic of who's left
after cancer has taken one in three

or, at our smartest, the bottom line
of a Magritte, the rest having risen).

On weekdays, with nothing on,
and the saint away from his hearth,

dust from the flawed cleaning rota
and ashes from the vandal's fire merge,

meaning even less in continuity
than each did before its solution —

this being our philosophy over the roast,
the antiphonal reply to faint praise.

Observer

Last week I caught Wilkinson masturbating
under soft light in Eichmann 1, juddering
at his boss's desk as if his seat were wired to the mains.

After leaving time I'd stayed at my post,
thrown the switch and drifted into a reverie
bordering on sleep. When I awoke and stretched,

I had a view of him from the wings:
a barking space commander piloting his ship
alone through a storm of asteroids.

I imagined his aerial performance
was for the wanking classes below us,
which reminds me that the video of choice

among our pork-friggers this month is *Stable Mates*,
in which two women cavort beneath a horse.
I suspect it offers the usual prelude:

the pair of degenerates arriving at a farm
on a motorbike and wearing hot pants,
followed by a forgoing of foreplay —

but no postlude (apart from the wobbling
of a bored video-operator and a blurred *exeunt*,
the pony led off sideways, hopping front to back),

an omission explicable on grounds
aesthetic and etymological, the film-makers
having neither a sense of shape nor access

to the word that might alert them
to its non-observance. Not even the story
of the great Catherine, wooden-caged

for a snorting Orlov-Rostopchin stallion,
would interest them, though it would underline
the difference between us, they with their lewdness

pure and simple and I with my extravagant take
on bestiality, and everything else for that matter.
Perhaps Wilkinson's wife was waiting for him

in their brick shithouse of a place on Lealand Road,
her face glum with boredom, maybe herself enjoying
a chipolata poke netherwards, and good luck to her.

The Elché Gardens

Books say this is where it happened —
stillness; doves grounded;
old men murmuring under the trees
of jousts with forgotten loves; wooers
simpering beside the jessamine.
Quickly a kiss conceals flesh
petrified by a death's-head hand
gliding innocently over it; and between
these matters done or unending
children come out to riot in dust.

Pock marks are preserved here:
buildings once flakked by rebels
are the corruption of a pure midday line.
Veterans groan at the tolled bell, thinking
it a summons to prayer and elegy.

Infanta at her Achilleion

They built me a palace on this land;
On this land, vistas rose to porpoise
Seas, mulattoes curved by statuary
Craved a footman's dispensation.
In my gardens, music combed cool vines,
Lamp-lit arbours, the pre-lapsarian
Dawn of whorls, fronds, plumed tufts.
Servants swayed to the cicadic click
Of an envoy's heels — and Doctor Lenz ran
Mad among us, scooping the air for
Drosophila melanogaster.

But in these rooms, Mister Zu and friends
Stripped to wax-white flesh in bedchambers
Among a strewn *décolletage* once
Sewn by hunched seamstresses; paragons
Sniffed like connoisseurs and rode on;
Warriors sought a swifter advance;
Emissaries declined. But Doctor Lenz
Hung around, for his quarry skeined
The fallen peach, emblem with fissured
Pediment of passage without root
To my deranged wave-engulfing oblivion.

Transporter Bridge

Mack the dispatch clerk makes
his leprous way to the jetty
for lunch. He likes me, the leper-lover,
because I'm like them, the earthsalt proles
back there, lining their lungs
with the sand from Petrankova's
thumping moulder (Petrankova,
who'd worked at foundries in Sofia,
Paris, Prague and Berlin, so he said,
and hated the lazy 'Engliss').

But once they knew my grandfather
had worked with them, I joined
their bronchial confederacy, the huddle
masquerading as the brotherhood of noise.
Gazing at the sheen on the river,
the gnomic Mack would invoke the harlot
while I saw my zealous grandpa and me,
dots crossing the bridge to subvert
his daughter's authority, my mouth
a protesting minnow's in a jam jar.

Circus Hungarica

Autumn once supervened for the stilt-man
to scan a swirling season, when soundless kids
tapped Morse through his legs.

Now, all presses in...

While Hercules blames space junk for the rain-ploughed sites
where his father, and *his* father, withered to feeders of seals,
Animal Madness scatters pictures of chained elephants,
dull tigers and bears at bay towards the palomino Mithras,
who rears, and ripples sideways at the bass hiss from Row G.
In Workington (Hary the driver had to finger it on the map),
they came wire-cutting in balaclavas to Pets Corner,
where Snow the albino fawn shivered on the edge of a freedom
spraying its light in rays.

After that, the menagerie, planned nose to paper
by old man Sagody at Kiskunhalas 'for the kids' sake',
was shunned at zoos and lugged around unseen till
death lightened the load or deals were struck
In the pearled Sagody caravan.

Buyers of marmosets recalled the line of
Sagody boys, their 'suite', the year turning early,
the leaning photographs of stallions high-stepping for princes.

When UR A Poet

A feather on the breeze
shall be a redstart's soul.

In the bedroom's dark,
objects shall emerge
as a tragedy on white paper
under the waves of a tilted tray.

You shall be vouchsafed
the hooded figure in black,
waiting to ambush old Mr Stiles.

Privy to the secret
behind the runnels of a prelate's brow,
you shall become a housemartin,
homing above the Loire's silver ribbon.

You shall question why
the Great War took so long,
considering how fast they walked;
see in the old-photo smile you wear
the wind made manifest
Among eddies and reeds. Finally,

impassioned, you shall imagine
what it will be like
when you have gone:
your form blurred at corners,
then lost among your memorials.

Roll Up, Roll Up...

I had Ricky to thank for finding myself
sitting alone in the front row of Zippo's Circus.
He'd walked out on girlfriend and young 'un,
and Josie had driven off with our kids
to visit her. I wanted the pair of them
to stay with me, but for some motherly reason
Josie insisted on taking them along.

We could have made it a threesome,
especially as the circus was one of those
without animals. The boys could have
learned some moral lesson. In any case,
I'd availed myself of Zippo's BTGTF offer –
buy two adult tickets and two kids get in free.

There we go.

It was a few years since I'd visited
the big top. I recalled walking
with my brother between the legs
of a man on stilts and hearing, far off,
the roar of lions and the elephant noise
whose name I can never remember. I also
seemed to have recalled watching
a juggler practise outside a caravan
and a thin girl in moth-eaten tutu balance
gingerly on a large pink ball. But the last two
may have slipped from my store
of the fanciful images we retain
from childhood or elsewhere: the pictures
of Picasso's *saltimbanques*, for example.

A lone male in a child's province
nowadays looks suspicious. It was
a sit-anywhere arrangement in the tent
and there were barely forty of us. So,

I was more than obviously exposed.
I wondered who Zippo was and imagined
him as the long-dead founder of a travelling
show indifferent to the issue of making
tigers jump through flaming hoops. I feared
being somehow short-changed.

First there was a tame trapeze act —
just routine swinging and catching
not all that high up — then a five-man
balancing team at ground level. One of them
had a hole in his tights.

Then a clown appeared at the entrance
to the ring and ran into the centre. He looked
my way and walked towards me
in his ridiculous, slapping boots. He came
up close and I could hear echoing laughter
as he pointed a gun at my head, fired it,
and showered me with confetti. Then
he put his face next to mine. Very close.

I saw anguish behind the painted smile
and felt — I am so sure of this — that he wished
to confide in me. A real tear, or dewdrop
of sweat, had lodged itself in one of the false
ones dripping from the corner of his eye.
The laughter of the crowd faded,
like daytime blotting up night.

Y FENNI/FISHPONDS

Sarno Square, Abergavenny, is the site of the former Pen-y-Fal Psychiatric Hospital, built in 1851 and closed at the end of the 1990s before conversion into flats. At its height it housed around 2,000 patients drawn from three counties.

There's a sister building in Fishponds, Bristol, formerly the Bristol Pauper Lunatic Asylum, where patients were removed to accommodate injured soldiers being shipped in from the Great War. The painter Stanley Spencer was an orderly there. After the war it reverted to its former use under a different name, and later closed. It is now the Glenside Campus of the University of the West of England.

I had to scrub out the Asylum Church. It was a splendid test of my feelings about this war. And I still feel the necessity of the war, & I have seen some sights, but not what one might expect. The lunatics are good workers & one persists in saluting us & always with the wrong hand. Another one thinks he is an electric battery...

Stanley Spencer, *Notebooks*, 1916

Diagnosis

Depression Guilt Hostility
Pity Remorse Disgust
Loathing Shame & Apathy
Boredom Fear Lust

Jealousy Suffering Wonder
Terror Desire Rage
Worry Loneliness Anger
Indifference Grief Old-Age

Dread Arousal Envy
Panic Horror Pride
Sorrow Phobia Misery
Terror Love Decried

Passion Hate Hysteria
Satyrasis Nymphomania

Melancholia Melancholia

Melancholia?

Melancholia

The Lunatic Act

They buried them in pits, singly
    or in pairs (the lovers Megan Lewis
and Cuthbert Rees), or in batches
    when the sweating sickness ran.
Records were kept: Victoria Hughes,
    'exposing her person, scolding onlookers,
paralysed, demented, parotid glands
    swollen, screams, sinks, dies at noon'.

But first Budding's rotormower, a jangle
    of parts swung through the weeds
to shave the first ten-by-twenty plot,
    a cartoon bubble with that wheel-in.
One quarter acre, they'd worked out,
    sixty-eight plots, twelve on each level,
four levels, forty per pit, the variable
    of sinkage, but room for at least three thou.

Precision! They craved it in that house
    of rude departures from the norm. Even
those gargoyles, defending the worsted,
    held their line as sculpted ironies.
Whoever entered — mimics dribbling
    and deluded (one said, 'I'm Fulljames,
the architect. Stable the horses!') —
    left stragglers, pieces of an endgame.

They'd done the arithmetic, established
    the categories of Abandoned and Leased,
so expected the odd brougham at the gate,
    collecting a corpse, sad epitome of peace.
But not Alice Hodges, her pupils
    dilating alternately, who'd left a reap hook
hanging from her husband's neck (all
    said the fool had 'ever made her mad'); or

the Isle of Thanet's Generalissimo – next
    to her in pit four, row three, level two —
who'd studied too much and eaten mangolds
    in a field of snow, but could play Baroque,
his piano a Weser light mahogany; and
    outside, *in extensio*, the Gothic, the Classical,
the Jacobethan, and the Doric — antidotes
    to the place's unbidden human rococo.

It went like this: first, the chapel service,
    an am-dram rehearsal, motley cast illustrating
religion's decline, much slouching in the pews,
    a Tourette's FUCK! at the Lord's Prayer.
Then a slither to paradise (just one hole
    dug to the storeyed incumbents), the Super
cupping a bivalve watch; the priest, fluttering
    angelus-like, smiling at the word 'committal'.

Day Book

Esme coopies and shits in front of the mayor.

Mrs Carroll's glasses have no glass.
She has secreted them again. They are
eyeing her through sunset in a pisspot.

Harold Chips again shielded from
Greta Febland, on account of her
24/7 celebration of Veneralia.

Mr Jarsdel is being pursued today
by a chanting mob; he buckles under
a cross and shrieks: *Ecce Homo!*

Gerald Hopkins, cornered, quotes
in Norwegian from Hamsun's *Sult*
but no-one will take him seriously.

Elizabeth Baines released, looking
beatific. Dr Baughan quips: *Satan subdued,
scales crackling, ember eyes aglow.*

Walter H's voices 'like Tewkesbury Market'.

Sailing from Delirium

In which a patient recovered from Concupiscence in 1899 seeks a new life for herself.

(With apologies to the shade of W. B. Yeats)

That is no country for a girl; the young
In one another's clasp, birds in the trees —
Those senseless generations – at their throng,
The doleful cries, the swarms of hopping fleas.
Mutton in slop for food all twelvemonth long
Then each begotten, ill, curls up and dies.
Caught in their crazy music all neglect
Examples of untroubled intellect.

A pensive lass is but a poor old thing,
A tattered coat upon a stick, unless
Nurse lifts her bell and rings, and louder rings
For every tatter in its haircloth dress.
Nor are there songs at dusk but studying
Monuments of their own indifference;
And therefore I have steeled myself and come
To father's birthplace of old Cheltenham.

O brothers standing in God's holy fire
As in Bethany Chapel's entrance hall,
Come from the holy fire, and lift me higher,
And be the sibling-saviours of my soul.
Consume my guilt away; sunk in that mire
And treated like a cowering animal
I knew not who I was; and gather me
Unto the loving arms of family.

Once free from terror I shall always make
My bodily form an undesirable thing
But such a form as pale novitiates take
In earnest prayer and heaven-bound carolling
To keep my love and heart in constant ache

For Jesu' Lord to whose pierced side I bring
My love, my all, my senses oh so numb
My past, my now, my found Elysium.

Would You Believe?

(*A Pen-y-Fal Nurse to her Husband*)

She bores him every day
with Who's In, and Things
You Couldn't Make Up.

He might as well be there
himself, she thinks, considering
how he never listens, or hears

wrong, answering, *Yes Please!*
to *Are You Feeling All Right?*
The latest cries non-stop, gone

from Grief afore it's healed him.
Tell Sanger's, the Seated One says;
and I *do* see him 'making a fortune'

in a tent with a horseshoe sign —
LITTLE WILLIE WEEPS:
NEVER STOPS A' SOBBING.

But, hands on his shoulders,
they turned him to the dark's door
and scratched him into the book:

Occupation: Porter
Admitted: November 17 1896
Condition: Melancholia
Name: Loveless, William John

Catatonia

Mr Maurice Rowsell, ex-
mortician, having seen off
his own life, stands naked
and asleep on his feet for
TWO HOURS, and is thus
the Artist's Model
par excellence.

Bit of a shock, though,
to limners imaginary in
the cheese segment facing
him full on, amazed

by the length of a dangler
unengorged and, knowing
the thing subdued, wondering
what it might be capable of
emancipated — or moderately
bestirred, like the life inside
a pupa, doing its Houdini act.

Little Mal, a Welshman

(Entered Bristol Pauper Lunatic Asylum, Blackberry Hill, Fishponds, in May 1901, aged 14; died there aged sixty)

Th' Approaching Air, in every gentle Breeze,
Is Fan'd and Winnow'd through the neighbouring Trees,
And comes so Pure, the Spirits to Refine,
As if th' wise Governours had a Designe
That should alone, without Physick Restore
Those whom Gross Vapours discompos'd before
..Bethlehem's Beauty, Roger L'Strange (1676)

Bowlie maestro thwacked
forehand and backhand when letters
arrived to say his twin brothers
had fallen at Spion Kop

Then real thwacks
from his onion-eyed old man,
who'd forged that iron ring
and the baton that stopped it
free-wheeling to the Darren

Whadya mean, yer stupid
mochyn, they couldn't get up:
they were bloody dead, mun

They'd find him, staring
at some Angel of Malakoff
near Paternoster Row, guided
him home, as if a blind kid

But he could draw. A shackled
alderman was unclipped to admire
his dragon, wax-crayoned on board

He learned Paardeberg, Majuba,
Ladysmith, Magersfontein — and
how to filch from Carmarthen Stores

*You'll have me in Abergavenny,
yerridiot, as sure as eggs;
you can bugger off to Brizzle!*

Fishponds Aunty Beatrice
took no lip, not even from 'the Cap'n'
squawking under a shroud. One day,
he freed him, sent him colour-flapping
along the Brentry Road, never
to be seen again (caveat entered)

Nor will you be, Bombazine
Bea rasped, after he'd wandered
three miles to view, unmoving,
Cap'n spiked atop the triton
of Rendall's Neptune (or pinioned
on re-surfacing, a first aerial catch).
It was said some prodded him
for 'all of' ten minutes, palmed
his ublinking gaze at nowt

*Nothing to be done? Nothing at all?
Nothing, your lordships. His father
be a Welsh drunkyard*

Etching him into the book, a clerk's nib
spits ink at his cheek. *You can rub it
all you like, sonny Jim, only carbolic
will shift it.* They were right.
Welcome to Blackberry Hill

*

Mal does not hear the babel of Black Tuesday

'As to our animal carved gargoyles
and other figures crawling over Doric
coursed squared rock faced Jacobethan
red sandstone rubble masonry snecked
to later work with plinth stringcourse
and Bath freestone', said Joe Beckford,
'watch me erect a tent in my trousers'

Mal misses out on the late massacre in Armenia

Stanley Spencer spoke up for Mal
when the Great War arrived leaving
the others to their refugee shuffle.
Mal sketched him going over the top
with a scrubbing brush, cleaning
hillocks, bangers (Mal never got limbs right)
and was despatched to find 'SS 1917',
not the trow known as *Marguerite*,
ploughing the Wye from Brockweir
to Portway and back, but his initials, carved
in the laundry, where Robert Staniforth,
('Too Intense Study'), mapping every inch
of the building again, came across them
the day Salazar's secret police sought sanctuary
from the baying mob. Stani bellowed,
Qu'est-ce que fucking c'est? and did not
expect, or wait for, an answer

The Frampton Cotterell Kaiser's latest: *Sack the boggers —
von Fluck, von Bulow, von Moltke! All the bally vons.*

Mal was humming *Myfanwy* to himself when Collins was ambushed

For a game of Hide 'n' Seek
not yet begun, Mary Taylor offers him
jam sandwich beneath the parachute
of her hand-me-down, wriggling
him towards a fetid place

Hugo Eckener, guest-flying
his Graf Zeppelin over Brizzle,
espies a field of fluttering folk
saluting the sun, their wild predicates
dissolved in the infinity of space. Mal,
'a pupil of Stanley Spencer', draws
a whale in the sky and its calf
on the ground, where it subsumes
Cuth Rees and Megan Lewis entwined
as well as seven members of the
five-a-side team, half kitted out

Mal missed the bullet that did for nephew Horace

The day Mr Chamberlain waved
his flap of paper, Mal was ill in bed,
watching Clara Beeseley struggle
to the furnace with towers of magazines
collected by the Super's wife: including
ancient copies of *Le Mode Practique*,
The Delineator, The Sketch,
De Gracieuse, and *Black & White*

Mal on his sixtieth read
the last crazy message (7. 7. 1947),
from morbid Flight-Sgt McConnell
to Albert of Brandenburg —
Over the rooftops
of Lauris, swifts
are re-enacting
the Battle of Britain

Mal in a trance didn't see death tip-toeing blindside

Janus

The two-faced clock tower
tells the wrong time twice
and chimes a third that's neither.

It stumps W. H. Creesey, horologist,
whose choral window display wears
one-fifty smiles and four-forty frowns.

Step up ex-miller Edwin Bor, poked
forward to correct it with a stare
after the example of Dr. Mesmer

on account of his ability
to hold off blinking for thirty mins
eleven secs, his record stopwatched

at twelve-two on 23/6/55; despite this,
it still showed three-eight and six-twenty
and tolled five when seven was bet on.

Terminus 1

The next train arriving
at Platform 3 will be the 4am
from Marne, Aisne,
Flirey, Arras, Armentieres

The next train arriving at
Platform 3 will be the 5.30am
from Gravensrafel, St Juliaan,
Frezenberg, Loos, Dickebusche,
Bazentin Ridge, Delville Wood

The next trains arriving at
Platforms 3 and 4 will be the 3am
and 3.30am from Langemarck, Gheluvelt,
Hamel, Chateau-Thierry, Soissons,

Amiens, Mont St.Quentin,
Havrincourt, Cambrai, Valenciennes

The next trains arriving at
Platforms 3, 4, 5 and 6 will be
the 5, 6 and 7am and 8.30pm
from Festubert, Champagne, Verdun,
Sambre, Neuve Chapelle, Bellewaarde,
Albert, Wulverghem, Flers-Courcelette,
Messines, Ypres, Mametz Wood,
Cantigny, Bellau Wood, Fromelles,
Pozières, Bullecourt, Lagnicourt,
Scarpe, Arleux, Pilchem Ridge,
Polygon Wood, Poelcapelle, Hazebrouck,
Kemmelberg, Scherpenberg, Ostend...

Terminus 2

They arrive by moonlight
    on the Mummies Express
so that Bristolians abed
    will not wake up to truth

Some hobble, some want
    to play pushchairs. A winding
cameraman decrees Silence
    like a ear-splitting *Feldhaubitze*

Advancing forever in a loop,
    the swathed sucking on pipes,
minding the gap, coming on,
    minding the gap, coming on

'Cheese' seeps out as 'Scheethe'.
    A few hover close to the lens,
a conshie's eye, but dissolve,
    like ethereal angels of Mons

At Glenside, the imbeciles
    have gone: dumb casualties
of peace making way for
    the deaf casualties of war

One photo shows a scattering
    on the lawn, the third still standing
after a whizz-bang has unleashed
    its skimming hell hounds; or

Those left (the seriously grim) beside
    their chairs after the music stops
for the sixth time in the Super's
    Don't Dare Smile competition

Notes & Observations

In the orderly room, they pretend
to play chess for posh visitors.
No moves have been made

Padded cell
a cheapskate
bouncy castle

Ward nurse glows at night, amid
her constellation of own worlds

Anne gives an ad hoc recital,
both pitches unsteady and imperfect

Bill Beesley, physio, on a visit
to the mortuary, tries on
Lund's Skull Coronet for size

Gert Parker's father 'always
carried a sadness within him'

Benny Smith's narcolepsy
barred by 'Mutt & Jeff',
the Dexy/Drinamyl two-hander

Maisie Wilhelmina Brockenhurst
('Monomania of Pride, with Epilepsy').
Question: Where were you born?
Answer: Mollycoddle
Question: Are you happy here?
Answer: Chicken's egg
Question: Where do you feel pain?
Answer: W. Tasker & Sons

Priscilla is sending a letter,
'guaranteed unopened', to
her chosen Judge in Lunacy

A loo called The Deluge

The town of Geel, in Belgium,
'welcomes the mentally ill'

A history of the hypodermic
syringe: chronology of pain
dwindling to a pin prick
never watched, scarcely felt

The chapel organist's repertory:
Elgar, Bantock, Wolf-Ferrari,
a deck of cards spread fan-like

Mr B can recite *In Memoriam*,
each verse chosen randomly

Mick and Montmerency:
straitjackets locked tight
in a glass case for display

Freddie M. shakes on the floor,
as if plugged to the mains;
his Dracula face post-prandial

The chess match begins: King
to dozing Queen's Rook Six; pawn
takes Bishop, Knight, Queen,
second Knight, in that disorder

Kingfishers In Puzzle Wood

There will be all sorts here: musicians, artists, poets – Thomas Royce Lysaght,
designer of the Bristol Pauper Lunatic Asylum

Only I in my folly know they are there:
against the green, pure Matisse; then

conclave of the technicoloured
by Milt Kahl and Woolie Reitherman,

work-whistlers. These Roman boulders,
dressed in moss, sprout bonsai to all

but a dwarf - tortured trunks like pangs
remembered, and branches they ignite

after diving - in each beak a broken rudd,
on each silvered rudd an eye, in each eye

reflections of others: fireballs tossed
into dank verdure. Mine, but a scary place,

voice of Lucille La Verne, voice of Adriana
Costellati. They flutter to a ledge, line up,

coo and bill. Pinto Colvig or Otis Harlan,
both uncredited, bring up the rear, peer.

That old time is too much with us. This is real,
this is unpredicated, this is Fauve.

Simple and pure, only I know it is there.
They scatter at no Prince's coming.

Patient Record: the Photograph

By bringing her home, I imagined
she might lose the misery shaping
her features, like Uncle Lionel did
when making a clown's sadness elide
to jollity in a downward sweep
of his hedger's raw right hand.

But no...

She leans against a vase, bringing
us to our senses with her loss
of sense: not the decisive moment
beloved of a photographer blitzed
by an infinity of split seconds; rather,
the only instance there ever was.

The One Light...

...is the Super's sleepless daughter, writing
to her sad Captain at Craiglockhart.
Though on the cusp of a visit — ten hours
and change at Crewe and Carlisle — she saw
his shivering simulacra from her seat
in the Electric Theatre, its newsreels
from the Front having long shamed the flag
and turned their dark pit darker, stalled
the hands that grope, drawn the sweetness
from their whispered nothings. 'They're away
with the fairies!' shouts some cowherd
six stunned rows down, as the screen shocks
with a couple of Accrington Pals mimicking
his old man's stagger home from The Feathers.

There's no name for it yet, the manic quivering,
the mouse-like scuttle under the bed, the pretence
to insanity. The one light, says the nyctophiliac
Dr Baughan, strolling the grounds at witching hour,
means the docked Titanic's Purser is palming coins
well before dawn and the iceberg's siren song.
True, she thinks, at night the Pen-y-Fal façade's
a cliff face, the side of an ocean-goer, all lights
dimmed bar hers; but she must get on, stymied
by how the pounding of a Paris-Geschutz at Ypres
has blitzed her Cap'n's fervid love to jibbering.

Gargoyles crowd the waterspouts; nightjars churr.
The doctor stops and seeks names for hysteria;
they will come, like the lone howls at midnight.

The Place

This is the place. You see the doves
and the blotched pigeons, ferals imitating
pale chastity and corruption, souls
of the ones who would never leave?

This is the place where they roost
and perform their broadbrush circuits
around the clock around the clock
that tells the wrong time. It's still home
to them, its boundaries invisible still,
a circus life subsuming high leaps
of trust. Here they come, inswinging
to a ledge in shadow. This is the place.

A hawk will hit a straggler grown
complacent of the ever-alert: see the blackout
between take and tear; the double squall
of feathers; the gang of magpies gathering.
Safely perched they neither know nor care
that one of them is missing: the bird-brain
brain of a bird is its own parameter, a sparkler
of instincts not to be disturbed; a threat
is a spiked synapse, not a hawk picture.

This is the place that was always taking
the mad dead away from the unknowing,
who for an hour were live statues, staring
at absences; or biting hard on leather
in the plush sanctuary, frozen in jackets,
turned from the world's careless turning.
Yes and yes and yes. This is the place.

*

Answerphone

Jim. Mike here. There was a message for you. From Jane. She said not to worry. And she'll ring as soon as poss. She did say poss – not possible. I mean she said just poss, not not possible. Just in case you are confused. By my message about her message I mean. I mean I wouldn't want to confuse you. Not where Jane is concerned. Especially not where Jane is concerned. That's all there was of the message. Jane's message. I nearly said Jim's message. Freudian slip, as those who've never read Freud always say, are always saying. Have you read Freud? I doubt it. I mean you probably haven't had the time, what with the unfortunate business with Jane and all. I suppose that's irony. I don't mean I doubt your interest in reading Freud or your capability of understanding him should you be bitten by the psychology bug. Now there's a stupid expression – bitten by the psychology bug! As though our interest in intellectual matters, things of the mind, is (I almost said are) akin to a supine state, a disinterested state, whose implicit lethargy can be transformed only by random stimulus. Anyway, there it is. Hope I'm doing right by you re. Jane. Since she went off the rails that time. That's why she's rung me. About you. It's what we said might happen. Remember? Even though the therapy hasn't finished, as I understand it. Her therapy. We didn't converse as such. I said I'd tell you she'd rung, would pass on the message, such as it was. That she had rung was actually the message, which obviously is mine, not hers. So there's only one message – mine. Her phone call, my message. She sounded, er, quite normal. I suppose it's the medication. Is she still on medication? I think by 'not to worry' she meant not to worry that you weren't here. Why would you be? She evidently thought you might. So she's still confused. As was I, am. Speak soon.

Muybridge's Runner

The money was in an envelope
leaning against the glazed vase,
the remnant of a house of cards.

The black drape was a flag for the world's
mourning, and his surly assistants,
waiting to unveil the secret apparatus.
They gave you your mad orders: strip,
and streak from left to right
as though your life depended on it.
Look straight ahead, they warned,
readying their moustaches
for his brisk entrance. You heard
Go! and a mechanical churning.

It was a frozen, temporary place.
You were glad to get dressed,
pocket your pay and return
to the pool, where he had first spied you,
a body trapped in the Turkish bath,
a head misted among echoing voices.

You ran from Jeremiah and Ezekiel,
vain pursuer and covered ankle,
to the arms of your lover.
You were the naked prodigal, racing
towards the arms of your father.

Wildlife

I've seen a lot from my window:
a siskin snatched by a hawk; woodpeckers
stabbing the lawn for ants; a fox
staring; badgers sweeping the yard.

O, inventories!...

Matters of
phyla , family and class, the plant
run down, the snipe's gut
dissected, mammalia,
mimicry, meiosis...

Once, when it began snowing
beyond the radiator and darkness
was engorging the day's spaces,
I let out a little cry: *Pee-loo, pee-loo.*

My wife is worried about me.
What was that? she asked,
her face crystal-lit in the next room.
Nothing, I replied.

Nothing.

Collecting Folk Songs

(*In memoriam Béla Bartók*)

Who this crazy come
among us now, with unicorn
apparatus and brittle cylinders?
And you, the photographer, ordering
us to be shot against the walls
of widow Szekely's house?

Look at Karparti's daughter,
how her pretty ditty cranks
his machine to a whir while
the young man takes notes — time,
place, date – and tears after
his butterfly of a tune
into the endless forests!

Rozsavölgy's hound couldn't care
a toss; swinging at another flea,
he'll be a brushtroke in the picture!

Austerity

(July, 1953)

On trips out in the Standard,
Uncle Ralph made up weird stories,
one with the following characters:
Erik the Kruel, Mr E. Gregious,
and the faceless ferryman.

A dark tale, like the cloud
tracking us to Cheddar Gorge,
stalling as we dropped down
in imitation of the slip of aeons,
to a windmill-whirring hell.

Dad still had his 'Monty's hack',
rough as the nylon brush he used,
but Ralph's hair was growing out
and over his jacket's quotation marks.

'Rear gunner OK?' my mother asked.

Ralph didn't answer, just kept
drawing on the steamed-up window —
Mr G, 'the Styx', a pitiless king.

The rear-view mirror was a little TV,
my father a newsreader looking anxious.

Schumann's Remedy

(Injured after using a quack contraption intended to strengthen his fingers, the composer Robert Schumann was advised to plunge his hands into the guts of a freshly-slaughtered cow)

He couldn't bring himself to look,
    just quizzically guessed the parts – liver;
stomach, ever gurgling, he reported,
    with a faint buzz, like the head
of Clara's cousin Wilhelm, still on the go
    after decapitation at the Battle of Leipzig;
and something small and knotty, alive,
    slipping into his grasp with the final rush
of a prodigal, and remaining there, lodged.

Naturally, they'd made a fuss. Not every day
    could they shut shop, stud starched collars
and buff up gaiters; though old Mendelberg,
    retired Chief Flayer brought back for the occasion
after an hour with an easy-sing version of *Myrthen*,
    still gave off the Slaughterman's Whiff.
Neumann said it was the first time he'd seen
    the cobbles fully dried out, a moot point
contested by the other Knifemen on parade.

One of Krause's time-served beasts was chosen,
    a doleful dame well past milking, now shuffled
with her dim bovine knowingness
    into the depopulated pens, the killing yard.
Something offstage signalled to Schmidt-Lange,
    Lights Man and pianist, the commotion
after the prelude, followed by the postlude
    of a dwindling cataract of blood. He alone heard
giggling bubble atop the knot of visitors.

Then the steaming carcass brought on
    and tipped to the side, the composer in it
up to the armpits (as Fischer the Offal Man joked),
    going for broke as if at his very own *Toccata*
but undecided on full tilt or light touch;
    not that the distinction worried Muller the Apprentice,
who had never come across Schumann and believed it
    when told how old man Krause's sacrificial cow
must in her time have given birth to a whole herd.

Marion Morehouse

(*to her friend Florence Herman*)

Everything depends
on Mrs Cummings

not getting rid
of the Remington

that maddeningly
won't type capitals,

notably the E and C,
among several others.

Kirkham

Against the river's flow we walked apart,
like Mr and Mrs Mickelberger when we were kids,

the gap between them widening along the cemetery,
the steep school yard, the black gully where

wild ground pitched them, relentless vanguard of the Diaspora.
But we weren't talking; just making light of distance

in imitation of the priory, with its longing porticoes
left out in the rain, divided, muzzled by time,

scaled by human statuary. You soon caught up
with me in the wood. An acrobat plane fountained,

stalled, plunged crazily; and the leaves, too, fell incessant,
merging us in the late acknowledgement of marvels.

Kempsey Murals

The Wests cruised past here,
not to pick up at those bus-stops condemned
to be ivy-climbers, but on their way home
via Much Marcle, where innocence, wreathed
in honeysuckle, glimmered dimly like
these pastel saints, who seep through
the once-effacing lime in still-stern attitudes
of love and stricture, their borne crosses
proclaiming the one who died for the many,
in contrast to the several who died so that two
less than a shilling could postpone redemption.

A smile wounds this place's silence,
its merging titter violates this hollow;
words jostle to make a point about as clever
as these dulled vestments are radiant.

Sam. Johnson in Uttoxeter

Fast-forwarded clouds of remorse
    overture the thunder of guilt
inside his temple as he remembers
    what was no more than a request
lost in the puff from a slammed volume,
    so like the explosion of spores
from a boletus (tiny fart in the wood),
    which he's read about in books,
Legoland bluffs of them, that he barely hears it –
    'Please would you hold the stall for me?'

He twirls late from his disobedience,
    much as another ragged-arse would,
postponing wonder and, above the city's roar,
    setting flora recalled above flora perceived.

Climbing out of his slough, he makes
    for town and his father's trestle.
Another's in charge but it's still hammocked
    by the weight of tomes since risen,
the souls of bodies corrupted to nought.

And for an hour he bears witness, head
    inclined — the odd tic for variety —
as they roll up to cheer the class act of homage,
    the demented penitent in the ring,
the rain-lashed whirlybird of contrition.

Bodoni Bold

(From a newspaper style book and a typographer's manual)

Artist (in studio or on stage);
By-election, by-law, by-product;
Cast (in play), caste (sect), coconut, consensus;
Dispatch, dram (not drachm);
Foregather, folklore, foxhound, flyer;
Gypsy; an heir (an RAF, an LMS);
Likeable; net (not nett), octet;
Quartet, quintet; sextet, nonet (not nonette);
Pigsty, pigsties, propeller, Peking;
Rateable; show (not shew), Sudan, saccharin; wagonette;
Yeti (not Yettie or yettie or yeti), yolk (egg), yoke (ox).

Mad dogs and English
Mad dogs and Engl
Mad dogs and En
MAD DOGS AND
MAD DOGS

Fleeing the Sight of Blood and Other Departures

Diverted from mundane and blinkered routines, we remember the unknown, the not-to-be-known, the puzzling. I had an uncle who died before I was born. The youngest of five children, he succumbed in his late teens to rheumatic fever. We begin constructing. Did I make it up or was I told that, as a boy in short trousers, he would accompany my paternal grandfather, his father, to the allotment in our Welsh valley where crops were being cultivated as a matter of urgency? This was during one of the miners' strikes of the 1920s, or it may have been in the Depression, when my grandfather, Grandpa Jarrett, a coalminer (or 'hewer'), was out of work. My father told me in his late, revelatory phase — intimations of mortality loosening the tongue — that had the table not been supplied with home-grown produce, the family would have starved, though he possibly said 'might', not 'would'. This short-circuits to my spectral uncle, running around the plot in the dampness of an autumn evening, his shirt billowing, while my grandfather, with typical male unconcern, bends his back to the easy art of digging, hewing.

I realise that such a construction implicates my grandfather in my uncle's death, a thought exacerbated by my grandmother's habit of running to the bottom of the garden whenever a crisis involving physical injury had been reached inside the house. Those were days when you could catch a cold, a 'chill', from exposure to low temperatures and the wet, and when the family provider often had a perch of land as well as a garden at home on which to work. I never got this story of flight from Granny Jarrett herself, probably because it connoted a weakness that, as a matriarch, she would have been too embarrassed to admit. Although to me a sort of madness, there may also have been only one example of it, magnified by repetition and embroidery into a myth of damaging over-sensitivity cancelled by a reputation for the intrepid that manifested itself later in her life. But we remember pictorially. I see my grandmother standing apart from the house after one of her sons, maybe my father, has accidentally skewered his hand with a pair of scissors. There is much blood from a disproportionately minor wound. She is quietly hysterical, paralysed by fear, anxiety and powerlessness, while a train approaches. Beyond the garden fence and atop the steep bank behind it was a railway line, one of the many closed in the 1960s by Dr Beeching. (I always smiled at the connection between his doctoral status and the economic surgery he performed; it must have suppressed the volume of outcry from an enraged but deferential public.) A few trains an hour, passenger and freight, steamed past.

Granny Jarrett it was who, late in life and on trains, had the odd habit of removing specks of dust from a grandchild's eye by licking the corner of a handkerchief, folding it into an arrowhead and gingerly scouring the eyeball for the offending mote. Since then I have associated steam trains not just with spotting them at railway stations but also with sundry grit, my grandmother's probing, the descent of the arrow (I had an Uncle Harold) and the smell of another's spittle. I assume that my grandfather resolved all these crises with sticking-plaster and a chuckle at his wife's momentary withdrawal, her eccentricity.

But I would have to bestow the chuckle as a formal element to complete the picture. To my knowledge, there is no photograph that shows Grandpa Jarrett smiling or otherwise enjoying himself — quite the opposite. Although his wife was from middle-class stock (her father was a self-employed builder from Somerset who constructed his own house and the terrace of which it was part), the home of a miner on the edge of the South Wales coalfield at that time, supposing it to have been unaided by beneficence from another part of the family, must often have been spartan, joyless even. My father's disclosure of its precariousness in times of want supports the view but also suggests that help from an expected source was not forthcoming, either through reluctance on the part of the giver or pride and stubbornness on the receiver's part.

This is where, in the absence of recollection, picture-making degenerates into speculative doodling and scribbling. So a few photos are not worth a thousand words but are all we have in exchange for them. Even at the seaside on a reasonably sunny day, Grandpa Jarrett's mind is on something else, something serious out of shot, perhaps the start of some commotion at the sea's edge that will turn out to be a drowning, the death of a child. I always remember him as a man of silence rather than a man of speech, a ruminative, saturnine character, not a demonstrative one. He once caught me, a fledgling smoker in the outside loo, puffing on a rolled-up page of the Daily Mirror. Typically, his admonition was specific — if I had to embark on a life as a smoker, I should wait till I could afford cigarettes — and the result of helpfulness aforethought. In some circumstances, one might have been afraid of him, wary of his inscrutability. But he was not physically a threat; in fact, he was a small man with a small, almost identical brother, with whom communication was either silent or the result of some disharmony or irreparable fracture in the past. His brother was never without a pipe in his mouth, and I always felt that it acted like a dummy did with a child in transforming any speech he contemplated into meditation and the sucking solace that went with it.

These scattered clues about my paternal grandfather lessened the shock of learning, when my parents' generation was passing away along with those of its predecessor who had lived well beyond their Biblical lease, that he had suffered some kind of nervous breakdown. In a family that never discussed much that was emotionally raw, the range of taboo was comically extended and allowed flawed individuals, myself included, to reach their apotheosis unless they were willing to postpone or banish it. It seems that Grandpa Jarrett, at some time when his children had grown up, disappeared for a lengthy period to stay with one of my aunts, both nurses, then living in the London area. It's all still vague, but it accounts for my grandfather's morbid disposition, something my father inherited to such an extent that there is continuity. I was told that my father, too, almost 'went under' during the second world war while working mercilessly-long hours as a vehicle mechanic to train service women in the use and maintenance of Army transport. It was a specific plaint, unlike my grandfather's, the vulnerability almost echoing my grandmother's headlong rush away from duty and disaster. (In me, the offending gene mostly sleeps, but is aroused now and then in an attempt to make me miserable.) In the case of my father and grandfather, there might also have been some guilt associated with not having gone to war when many of their friends and neighbours must have: a reserved occupation could never have been a substitute for a heroic one, despite, in the latter's case, the deification of the labourer. For sure, their journeys towards the waving weeds of the depths, those emblems of silence and ghostly melancholia, might, in less sympathetic families than theirs, have seen them end up, for a time at least, at Pen-y-Fal Psychiatric Hospital in Abergavenny. Every misbehaving son and daughter knew the threat of being responsible for their frazzled mothers' possibly ending up 'in Abergavenny'. There's a little madness in us all, not least those who put the maximum possible distance between domestic calamity and their duty to confront and subdue it. To have abrogated responsibility for something that led to serious injury or worse might have led to committal.

Which leaves me with the legacy that both nags and consolidates: the only picture I have of my parents' wedding. It's a semi-candid, post-ceremony shot, like the eccentric image of an Impressionist, with my maternal grandmother in the distance, hand on hip, and the bride and groom kneeling with one aunt and one uncle — my father's sister and brother — standing behind and not smiling, their attention caught by something beyond the frame, such as a child in danger or the threat of impropriety from a returning prodigal. Directly at the camera, and down the years, my father with his creased brow stares at some indefinable anguish, already present or yet to be. He does not smile. It is not the look of a regular groom, buoyed by goodwill and congratulation and blushed by expectation. My mother does smile, and thus resembles a bride from some other, less fraught, ceremony.

All this leaves my mother and her parents, as far as I can tell, free of the taint of neurosis, and working-class without any intervention of a middle-class element in the shape of a Somerset master-builder. Without complication, especially the tantalising sort never to be unravelled, there can be little scrutiny, not even of the effect Granny Jarrett's apparently supercilious attitude to my mother's betrothal had on their future relationship, something my mother, in her own way, said was due to class consciousness, though she never used that expression. In any kind of hypergamy, and the opposite in my father's case, one side gains and the other loses. What persists is resentment. Although my maternal grandfather was also a miner, and after that a foundry labourer, everything about the two families illustrated low-key but telling class difference.

My mother's parents lived in a house that in the 1970s and afterwards would be ruled uninhabitable. When pensioners, they moved into sheltered housing, though my grandmother was always semi-disabled, again from some injury or complaint that arose after her picture was taken at that conjugal assembly, when she looked elegant in a matronly sort of way. Later on, they were poor, while my father's parents stayed a pitch beyond poverty's shadow. Even so, there were points of contact and mutual concern, not least the levelling of those wintry recessions in the 1920s. I remember accompanying Granny Jarrett each Saturday to 'the Death Club', a Methodist chapel institution which collected money to defray the contributor's funeral costs. It was an exercise of prudence in the land of the doom-laden. I would have been as tall as the exchequer's trestle table and its piles of pennies. She shared with my mother's father an ability to play the organ, though this would have originated in the Edwardian practice of providing homespun family entertainment. I may be wrong or forgetful, but I cannot remember the two families enjoying any sort of regular social contact, even though they lived almost within the same square mile and, the devotional ones anyway, attended the same chapel. (Incidentally, the schisms among Non-Conformist denominations in South Wales were often as striking as the one between Anglican 'low' and 'high' church. The hysteria, clinical in many cases, worked up by the Religious Revival of Evan Roberts and others, was its historic concentrate.) Perhaps, in the striving upwards and outwards at that time, one had to be self-interested, and sensitive to the weight of baggage.

I visited Grandpa Lang, my mother's father, when he was ill and had not long to live. I asked him how he was, and he answered, 'Not too good, son.' I always found that use of the word 'son' to be a distancer, a means of familial disengagement. And I always recall the pained look he gave me afterwards; it was compounded of his own internal agony and probably the contempt in which he held any slippage from grace – again, something not to be talked about or confronted directly. It would be tempting to view his lapidary working-class position as a commentary on the two characteristics I associate with him: his reputation as a disciplinarian, and his later manifestation as a subversive. Although unbecoming for a man in his mid-seventies, and thus concealed, he'd been an occasionally violent upholder of parental authority. My mother and her four brothers told of the leather belt he kept hanging by a hook on the kitchen door to be used against them if they defaulted. And it was used. Whether or not the placid demeanour of my mother and uncles was a result of this tyranny would be hard to say. But, as his young grandson, I experienced its eclipse and dilution. When I was eight, he would take me to nearby Newport, a docklands town with a see-through transporter bridge – one of only two in the country – and a covered market. We would go first to the bridge, not crossing on the suspended gondola but up scores of metal steps and along the top, my little mouth an 'O' in the gale. It was popular with suicides. At the market, he would buy me things of which, he knew, my parents would disapprove, such as a 'potato' gun (you shoved the end of its barrel into a potato and fired starchy pellets) and a catapult. My parents and others tut-tutted, and thus was the loss of his old dominion partly assuaged. I never squared this mischief with his position as chapel organist. Like most of the congregation, he listened to the preachers, but never discussed religious matters with them.

Nana Lang, being eternally seated by the fire, would wield no such influence. Over her shoulder, through the window, I could see the outside loo – and the L-shaped chicken coop, where I would cup the warm china eggs placed in the straw to encourage the hens to lay. Nana Lang remains in my mind as stationary. It's only now that I marvel at the mechanism of how, when no-one else was there, she got about on walking-sticks, and the part that her labouring, belt-twirling, late-insurgent husband played in it. He had an allotment on an elevated site over-shadowed by the mountain, Mynydd Maen, that he had entered with Grandpa Jarrett and others to hack at the coal face after a three-mile journey. This was an adit mine, not a deep shaft. (There was more than one way of getting at the 'black gold' in Wales.) Once, he took me to his allotment, maybe to see the transporter bridge in the far distance after one of our visits. What he particularly wanted to show me was the valley level below, scarred and trampled by earthmovers preparing the ground for one of Britain's new towns. It looked as though a mythical titan had been writing messages on the land, the churned earth red as blood. If he'd had the words he might have said, 'There you see it: the New Jerusalem.'

For the grandparental quartet, such concerns have long been over. For us who remain, lack of knowledge has been due in part to generations of reticence, when the taciturn triumphed, at least among those who stayed at home all their lives and, it appears, fought off demons. My father was a talented amateur artist, like his older brother; my mother was a lifelong choral contralto; Uncle Peter, he of that fateful frolic in the damp, and dead at seventeen, wrote letters to the *Radio Times* and was learning the violin, his instrument being buried with him. In another time and in other circumstances, their ratio of talent to achievement might have been different, but in many ways its power of revival and reappearance is strong. I try to imagine Nana Lang, perennially aproned with a large front pocket, reaching for a mobile phone that would have partly transformed her existence; and my father, practical by virtue of some insistent gene, taking but a day to master computing.

Most of all I try to banish thoughts of estimate based on social position, which I've always believed to be a kind of derangement. My maternal grandparents strove only to survive at a more-or-less subsistence level; my father's parents, with survivor skills possibly encouraged by a self-made go-getter from the West Country, must have felt the stirrings of mobility, the dim glow of a distant field day, possibly as a result of genetic input. My father was first a motor mechanic, then an insurance agent. Economic and social advancement often involves, on the spear side, the gradual disappearance of dirt under the fingernails, and is often prey to maddening frustration. The whole family were Methodists, but my father had long opted out of weekly worship, only to be cremated following a Christian service in the chapel where he'd also been married: a prodigal's return. I and my siblings didn't last long under that Non-Conformist roof either; and we've made other arrangements for our obsequies. It could be progess but it might be simply change; a diversion, *gwyriad*, from paths not to be taken, obstacles not to be faced, opportunities not to be grasped, regions not to be explored. — *Hic sunt dracones.*

Spinsters

How could we forget them?
    Estranged,
they bickered between floors
of a steep, symbolic dwelling:
'She' in the street-level shop,
'Her' mangling and mumbling below —
their counting-house and powerhouse,
impregnable against the incursions
of soft-spoken, Brylcreemed men.

On Sundays they paraded their
    sisterhood,
scaling the alpine stairs in silence
and silently parting at the bridge
as Pisgah and Siloam beckoned,
those unwilling accomplices sundering
an alliance, little knowing
that division ruled, even after
the eyelid blinds had closed.

What sealed their unity
    of intent,
sliced them from a sibling legion
the same way 'She' palmed bacon
on to greaseproof sheets?
We were too young to know,
mesmerised by the rising sap
of a hymn which fixed them,
two lissom trees swaying.

Perhaps as young women they had
    formed a pact
to stand proud of fecundity,
the corruption of lust and deceit,
of pit lives reaped so cheaply.

Except for a slow inkling
that pride was indivisible,
they may have found comfort
in the shared consciousness of loss.

Siloam shunted Pisgah for the
    funeral
before 'Her' coffin was wheeled in
to a tune 'She' shamelessly descanted.
By then we had ceased to be
Sunday afternoon surrogates;
and 'She', too, was not long
for that house, vertiginous
with offspring of bitter memory.

Galatea

An indifferent god scars
the face of the sinner,

stamps her lipstick awry,
overdoes the eyebrows,

befools modesty with slap-on lashes,
dyes the hair a hellish yellow.

I know this from my visits
to Aunty Dora, sad dweller

of the margins for wedding
a lag, who thunderbolts

into the hall as we sip tea,
skeined by chintz light.

She will never leave him.
Her perfume is liquor —

a miasma near her head,
a harbinger of his surfeit.

She has driven him to this,
her rivals safe in Capel Sion.

As she stands midstream,
he is floodwater, writhing at her feet.

Mobile Snax

Our little daughter Indigo
(we are the Beat Generation,
flower-powered, caked
veterans of Glastonbury)
says the cabin's happy
when I split the shutters,
is glum when I close 'em,
and me and the missus
are Punch and Judy inside,
serving the men who lean,
dwarf connoisseurs, sniffing
black tea like Bisto twins.

Talk of the wife, hours,
the road sliding beneath them
like a reeled-in belt.
The wind lifts their hair,
these grey men, and the sun
blinds their talk to mouthings.

Comes the flame arc-ing
across flesh and element,
sausages jigging into life,
cataracts clouding fried eggs.

Midwifery

Remember that hoar day
    (you couldn't possibly forget)
when they took your phial
    and injected two Mallorcan toads?
They said one was a control
    to ensure some aberrant prick
didn't make the warty varmints
    sprout eggs out of spite.

The unlucky one squirted a result
    while we slept like cupped Geminis
and, I fondly imagined,
    the flax-dam Irish cousins
slopped and plopped threats.

We did duty before the registrar,
    but now you frolic elsewhere
with two who detained no amphibians:
    Alytes obstetricans, as old as the Triassic,
like memories under all that weight.

Saddo

I'm in cuckoo love with the woman
next door. Her billowing semaphore
confirms it – the bedspreads,
sturdy metaphors for passion, fecundity;
two bras yes, one no; a line
of tights asking if I mind about
the others (well, I don't, promiscuity
being part of her attraction).

There is, of course, the cat basket,
soggy at first, chevronning the line,
a single, maddening consideration,
then flimsy and drip-free.
It reminds me of her domestic side,
like the socks, a team's-worth,
indicating him indoors, the boulder
in the path. I'm waiting, though,
and so is she, the taut filament
signalling a pause or, knowing my luck,
the neon blips flattening out, marking
a sweet, sorrowful end to it all.

Promises

Come down, he said. We can listen to
    the nightingale.

Funny, she thought. He'd never been one
    for birdsong.

I'll sleep, he added, on the settee; if that's
    what you want,

meaning, she knew, that his martyrdom
    would follow her reluctance.

But at least, she felt, there'd be something new;
    in the moonlight apparently.

We should go, he explained. Sometimes
    it's there, more often not.

Here we are, he announced. It was a ritual clearing;
    but the ranting moon didn't show.

Nor, she needn't have added, did the nightingale.
    He followed her back.

Any Savlon? she asked. I've snagged myself
    on some fucking bramble.

He spoke in his sleep, she recalls — tortured stuff,
    so he was probably awake.

She opened a book, he noticed, specs perched,
    knees up, tush a full set monty.

Cold Comfort

A thaw
    made the top snows
come clean

concerning
    earlier impressions
of yours —

solidified
    trampling, scuffles;
the trail

led off
    to nowhere,
though doubtless

a virgin fall
    awaited fresh
markings.

A frost
    prettified you
before melting

like memory loss
    or the veiling
of a deception.

Art

(*Bring something personal along; anything*
— poet's injunction to workshop students)

A video of that drip at the end of the tap?
It hangs there for ages as if in a film
about a glassblower by Andy Warhol.

Or one of *Alandale* now that Dora's gone
away and forgotten everything? It's a Whiteread,
its memories displaced from inside.

A sketch of Uncle Jim after that migraine,
when he furrowed at the Cubist portrait
and the Dali watches of his Pontefracts?

What about the tile I kept when I should have
fixed the wall after a year's crumbling delay,
its back a Mondrian (I was filling in the grid)?

There's always the passport pic you flung my way
after toeing it out like a spent fag:
it's a Bacon — me twisted in a hall of mirrors.

The Wilmcote Plesiosaur

Museum-ed now, its bones
stuck upright on a board,
it might be clinging to Velcro,
sent flying by son-of-the-town
Randolph Adolphus Turpin
and caught in that precise
Desperate Dan moment
when it smacks against the wall,
leaving a draughty forensic
of having passed through.

Violence is frozen here:
Turpin's 'put-'em-up' statue;
dinosaur feeding-frenzies;
tomb violations; heaving aeons
in candy stripes; Friday night blood
at the door; wormed ducking-stool;
slave testimonies; arrow tips in bone.

And we, too, are being counted out.
Having come this far, rages stilled,
we mimic Randy's pretence of fight
still in us, aimed even at each other
when punches are pulled and we'll stop
only at a moment like this: I turn
from the Plesiosauran's skyward swim
to find you gone; and from upstairs
the Great Warwick Fire crackles down
amid distant wailing and commentary.

Persephone

She was ever the sober one, fleeing
    the shadow of his late 'difficulty'
on days out with her gang
    and returning with one more exotic
for her festoon of prizes from beyond
    the borders. Hidden among them now
their Pre-Cambrian joint purchases:
    the stone cat from Appleby; the thyme
pinched by a local seedsman in Castellina.

That 'pathetic phallus' joke she coined
    reminds him of her now. He weeds religiously,
ticking the timetable over half-moons.
    Cystus flowers on the lash stare glassy-eyed
before falling over at midnight unseen.
    And there's that high-ground guardian,
old jasmine, its perfume a spectre's presence.

Orchard

A movement in the grass
where none had been;
an apple, gouged by birds,
slipping earthbound.

Each and both conspire
to prompt the obvious:
expulsion from Paradise,
Masaccio's vision
of coitus rudely nipped.

Yet it's Newton at rest,
struck by a law unbidden,
that lights my place —
not so much innocence lost
as the awful tendency,
signalled by rot and leaf fall,
of everything to run down.

Gold Watch Scenario

No clockwatcher, he watched the clock
for years until they cast him
from their half-hour of apportioned jollity –
one he could see at ten-to-six,
perhaps scrambling towards the finish
for fear of being late home again
and forfeiting a weary, wearied love.

The trick now is to stall it
with the help of daytime TV
(That pyrrhic victory of supply over demand):
but the bountyhunter bides no time,
swift Montana rivers bleed more colour,
the epic is a carrier of its own fall,
presaged in the fissures of Flintsone capitals.

He's kept his old man's toolbox,
its Steradent tubes heavy with drill bits
or full to the cap with candle stubs.
(What the fuck were they for?)
Maybe WD 40 can stop the corruption
of the retractable tape-measure,
which wants to curl up and die.

On the shelf under 'Lives of Others',
Proust gazes peevishly from the spine
of Hayman's biography, freed from
a library stock sale, never to be read.
What's to be done? Snow flints the wind,
soon to take his impress, the footfalls
of times past that brook no remembrance.

Gland

(*A Male Thing*)

Another letter makes it
Prostrate. I wish.
It's night's mischief-maker,
Clubber's engorged eye inviting
Me to the dance-floor time
And again. But this is more
Deserted ballroom and I'm its phantom,
Gliding through the gloom
Before my time but after the final
Crowd surf. Half way, I sit,
The Thinker, making
A weak
    tinkling
        protest.

Dying Now

Dying now at eighty, they were once immortal,
    as pictures at the time show:
hairstyles Vidal modern; a Bailey's skinny *hauteur*
    stopped short of disdain;
the attitude of a life lived in glittering parallel with ours.
    Even the earnest ones had finish,
unflappable in a flap, unstoppable in quests that seemed poised
    on the glistering blade of style,
the hemlines just so, the features native, untouched, the shoes —
    oh, the shoes! — so vocal.
Gushing obits brook no decline, re-live the tempo
    surrounding the photograph's decisive moment,
'tremulant twixt shirt and skin', blind to winging chariots —
    and surely eclipsing our vagrant
down at Christmas, who looks a bit like John Berryman
    moments after he called Rilke 'a jerk':
in the face, that whirling mixture of self-righteousness
    lanced by regret, to give him the benefit
of the doubt he's raised among the shop girls knelt in supplication
    around his head. Some head, too, marinating
in its aura of booze; Hunter's Moon eyes; the beard's origins
    indeterminate, destination unknown,
iodine-tinctured at sites of tippled poisons. And the digits,
    a seamstress's, wax-white, built for precision —
if the inside forefinger were not charred, its neighbour's
    dipped-in-sherbet impression the brand
of the extinct sixty-a-day man, now past intimations of mortality,
    an unknown facing slippage on an iced declivity.

Sylvia's Eleventh Hour

What if a diddy'd called to say
    he could do a proper job
on her railings, fifty quid,
    forty — go on then — twenty,
and no questions asked?

Irish, of course, exponent
    of blarney from the land of Seamus
and Kavanagh; but now
    with a voluble foot in the door
while the rest stand waiting

beside a Vesuvius of steaming tar,
    dying to know what's keeping Mick,
who behind her can see two kids
    premature in PJs, and gets a whiff,
dontcha know, of something not quite right.

Pet

We knew from the last time
how it would go: extinction

drawn from a phial into
a junkie's throwaway sharp;

shaved paw held in greeting;
the absence of premonition

as the death-dealer deals; and death
coming quick, coming quick.

And, dealing done, the back turned,
as if on a lewd or defiling act,

for us to contemplate a glazed eye's
agony stilled (our private moment).

Funnily enough, we thought of
Uncle Jim's 'single to Switzerland'

for when the time came, like us
encumbered with knowledge

yet selfishly craving the bliss
of both knowing and not knowing.

Pale Namibian Roses

Have you noticed
how flowers are replaced
only when they're over?

Not for us the despatch
in late but full bloom
out of boredom or caprice.

We await petalfall, waterwhiff;
the decline oblivious of fights,
cupidity, all weathers, absences.

Even the pale Namibian roses,
their scent and prick
sacrificed to a longer span,

are left to go reluctantly,
still compact with inbreeding:
lifeless in life come now to death.

Most of us reflect this; others
are tiger-lilied, ever staining;
a striptease their mode of exit.

A Memory Seat at St. Ives

Every summer and out of season they'd walked
   to Clodgy Point, ignoring the death ship,
thinking it an old Seine boat — pennants flapping,
   vague sea-picnic semaphore — ploughing its six-a-day,
there-and-back voyage to Seal Island —
   mostly no seals, despite the skipper's decision
to cut the motor and let the trippers switchback
   on swell, silenced, bar his old-salt snigger
and the gulls' hunger, by a sudden immensity.

   They'd done all that in the sun the first time,
before there were others: the kids, and *their* kids;
   the old man and woman watching them, stilled
by deckchair recall; friends leaving the building;
   jolly doctors with 'Perhaps, 'Maybe' or 'I'm afraid'.
They'd made wet prow and fish waves upstairs,
   safe from the Primitives and their missionaries,
tossed the wedding bouquet from Smeaton's Pier,
   watched it float, a wreath on jade waters,
to the lighthouse, then sink among mackerel.

   The first year they missed coming he was marooned
with another, a mermaid among waves of blankets
   and white-horse sheets at *The Navigation* — 'mermaid'
after her way of doubly crossing the typist's legs
   he would unfurl and spread wishbone-wide,
the skin of her skirt sloughing upwards in wavelets.

   Then, one day, she wouldn't make it; he cried,
posted her 'missing believed drowned' and rowed back
   to his own, waiting for him hand in hand on the cob.
His wife went first, against the odds, leaving him
   alone in Widows Avenue, where he became Fuse King
and Lord of the Jump Leads. It was in '87, summer
   of the Great Storm come snarling out of the night,

turning Porthmeor's surfers to dunces on the shore.
    He couldn't imagine that boat making it, and dreamed
of an explosion of sea lions, a spiteful gathering
    of blubber ringed by tern, shag and sanderling —
and slaps of water from bobbing harbour presences.

    He drove there alone one anniversary week,
to a Porthgwidden flat with a view, and wondered
    if the *Espanola's* captain, safe from sucking the depths,
had caught him in his glasses, helmsman in a land lashed
    by isobars on route to calmer things. The next day,
Clodgy ahead, he gave in, so missed the landbound tack,
    the low moans on deck, the change come over Captain Birdseye —
and, not to be lived through, the going-on of others.

No Upper Chain

Just moved into a place with things
I don't need: a wall-mounted bar
at the door to help me heave myself
into the house; a Sellotaped note
beside the cooker reminding me
to turn off the gas; some wooden steps
for climbing in and out of the bath;
a cat flap; a marble-mint mothball,
maybe dropped while someone
was scooping an armful of clothes.

I don't know about the garden
out there, whether to let the bamboo
and berberis strain towards an absence
in their fluttering and fire-berried acts
of extension or cut back to make new.

Whatever, the flap will have to go.
I wonder if the mog who crashed
through it night and day, slowly forming
that opaque arc at point of contact,
went first or was the last to go, flicking
the mothball into a corner before it,
too, was swept up; and I begin
listing what I really need: a blowtorch,
a wallpaper steamer, a doorbell
playing some hip tenor-sax riff.

Here Lie Loved Ones

I was about four feet down, almost there,
when my first came. I could see him,
her old man, turning left, left, right and left again,
picking his way between the green mounds
to announce, a Gulliver silhouette on the brink,
It's a boy, just as my downward pick split the point
where Florrie Carter's forehead should have been.

You didn't sweat in a green mac by the bed then,
playing doctors, looking down the valley
you'd fumbled in blind at a bloody mushroom
coming up for air in dark leaf-mould stench,
close to the miracle but really a speck on a hill,
like trying to guess the tune from the lyric
or a stuttering dumbo describing a beauty he'd met.

It was my first re-open of the week, a mucky job
while Len was dynamiting on the lawn, Row J,
(burial in virgin soil), an aeon from the two Carters:
him first, Redvers, waiting for the others to pile on top
then old Flo, almost a child's length (shorter than him
anyway) and now Harold, prodigal re-united at eighty,
sixty years a-wandering, deaf to plea and stricture.

Stealth outwitted the ward sisters that night;
been at the bedside since three, just staring
at the sick little thing, yellow in the crook of her arm
and her looking down pretending there was no jaundice,
no reason to be in that side room where I overstayed
my visit before waving, a voyager on the cusp,
her old man eyes front, a taxi-driver tap-tapping.

The vicar let slip Harold was Harry to everyone
(this from Len, listening at the chapel door
to signal us, Hawaiian trio sacrilegious in false-grass aprons).
Those neat stragglers didn't seem like pals, though,

coming at my grave from all quarters, the living dead,
hands clasped behind backs, as if hiding late gifts.
Sizeable Harold only just made it. Len winked. Closure.

Guillotine

Hubert spirals to the tower's point,
    his insect tripod tamed at arm's length,
for a view through an arrow-slit
    in the realm of the bribed custodian.
And fools – M. Leclercq, pupil of Daguerre,
    mocks a world of moving citizens
mesmerised; but Hubert has captured
    the brothers Montgolfier – they come
at him jerkily, lit by smiles, in exchange
    for a flight levered in hot air and wind,
and their shadow oozing across Paris.

But now this courtyard *coup de force*,
    as the insect is unleashed, trapped
in the unpeopled Chateau d'Allemonde.
    Hubert braves the slicing draught, tilts
the box, finds the view — and winds.

It's done in an instant. A breeze
    flags shirts and coat-tails. Headless,
the body slumps, attempts a scramble
    sideways; a grim magician clicks a finger.

But Hubert keeps winding, lingering
    on the space and time that follows
the event; a reproof to old Lerclercq,
    a void nascent with screams, sequels.

Kicking Leaves

(*A Mother's Plaint*)

He'd have been thirty tomorrow,
    kicking arse, kicking against pricks,
kicking a Sunday League football,
    admitting he kicks himself now
for saying No to that lovely girl.

Leaves are falling late this year:
    no quick frost to let them go.
It's called abscission, word entailing
    scissors and abscess, before scar.
But today I had to cast him off,

because my winter has officially come
    and ice has turned me inwards.
When Fall is finally fall I'll watch
    gusts scuff a few — sun-surface eruptions —
as he used to: here, there, here again.

Symbol

Each year after she left us, the cactus
she bequeathed continued to flower
at Christmas, thus mimicking
with its red blooms (that's if
the kids didn't nip them first)
the tearful tree, cornered like a dunce
and regaled without merit among
votive offerings, the best hidden till last.

This year it didn't go out for summer
or receive the manna of nourishment.
So, come September, when I looked in passing,
the gloss, its proclamatory sign, had gone,
meaning that, as the vicar noted ironically,
it would burst with the eastern star
and thus fall beyond its target, a memorial
to mark the first slippage of memory.

At the Crem

They said there wasn't much of him left
afterwards and that he'd been re-built
as a kind of half-decent Guy Fawkes,
like the ones who used to lord it over
Maesgwyn bonfires in the Fifties,
their power bases put to the torch
by Austerity's sappers, their pretence
of might falling into the wind
bit by flaming tattered bit.

And cynical fancy flows...
Remaindered Book of the Dead.
Encomium guy lying through his teeth.
Daughter's pathetic poem.
Pretending you know Crimond by heart.
Bad-joke ghost working the curtain.
Bread queue of the bereaved.
White chrysanth DAD proclaiming too much.
Don't mention the smoke.
How to sort Mr Smith from Mrs Jones?
And the oven-dodger's cartoon 'Thinks' bubble:
Let's be having you — the next one's up in five.

Care Home

Barney's at the window again, looking
    for his other names; or anything really:
the wedding day, or the evening
    she had to be told it was all over.

Behind him's no help, just that crescent
    of slumped traitors executed as they sat
while the harpist played on, oblivious
    to the clink, clink of their falling tambourines.

Yesterday he had his first full house
    but didn't shout it. Look! – those crows
are strafing the whatstheirnames again,
    them circling to heaven. Buzzards.

She's due to today, with the other one;
    and here's the bloody sky-pilot in his Merc,
so there'll be a 'Dickhead!' to be pocketed
    and The Old Rugged Cross to chivvy.

He can laser through the wall to the place
    — the thingamajig — where the Phyllosan's mixed,
burnt fish fingers are scraped, and plastic cups
    are pinged with their tiddlywink tablets.

Yonder the motorway's moving silver strip
    and the blue unremembered hills. You see,
he taught English and can still falsify
    Housman to the poet's invited detriment.

But he took his walking stick to whatsisname,
    the big fella, some Shropshire lad with a lisp;
they pinned him to the floor and he was crying
    out for home and the occupants he'd lost.

Now, here's a new 'activity': Efface the Face
    with mask and shield and Poke the Epiglottis.
PPE — three letters standing for what they need
    but haven't got, like the meaning of memory.

The Running of the Deer

Rounding a bend, we see it: a car
    squashed and steaming against a tree;
and inside, the driver, alive but agog
    before a windscreen starburst, the blood
imagined, panicking on route to the brain
    at some impediment finally come good.

The ambulance radio talks of crisis
    to no-one and everyone: a girl precipitate
on a bridge; a pummelled wife left
    for dead; a widower down, feeling
the draught from under the door rustle
    a stray hair, his thumb tabbed to a bleeper.

Now this; but distant on the park's slope,
    a herd of young roe, each dappled flank
luminous, every glazed snout afire, all heads
    turned as one to our cotton-knot commotion.
It quickens the fast-beating heart, the hoof's
    split tension, the shoal-like twist and scarper.

Alzheimer's Castle

You couldn't recall who likened
the gap between remembering
and forgetting and remembering
to a sheer butterfly's wing;
but that Lysandra Blue
raised and lowered the bridge
connecting the mined citadel
to the scent of hills and acres.

Then it died unseen;
all happened behind your back,
when its wings were one
and the doomed courtiers arose:
Aricept
Exelon
Reminyl.

They attend you now.

Ward C4 West

The nurse ran after me,
waving the miniature fan.
It went to the bottom
of the bag, so pathetic
had been its pretence
of reviving my father.

Now the sun pins me
feverish against the wall
and I dust the thing down.
It yelps and sweeps,
seeking the old man,
like an abandoned mutt.

NOTES

Like many other Welshmen who speak only English, I am seduced by mellifluous Gwalian words and phrases. *Gwyriad*, meaning diversion, is properly applied to roadworks signs, but I have used it metaphorically to indicate paths not taken, or, if taken, then leading to confusion and/or catastrophe. There is, of course, no way around the ultimate and universal destination, referred to several times in the latter part of this collection.

The Wilmcote Plesiosaur: Randolph Turpin (June 7 1928 – May 17 1966) was the undisputed world middleweight boxing champion.

Another place: 'Gormley's men' are the life-size statues in cast iron created by sculptor Antony Gormley and lodged randomly in the sand on Crosby beach, Liverpool, to remain at the mercy of corrosive tides and other elements. They may be an ironic comment on humanity's futile attempts to consider itself immortal.

Y Fenni/Fishponds: It would be easy to appear voyeuristic about psychiatric hospitals, particularly when they were called lunatic asylums. Even then, 'asylum' meant sanctuary, as it still does in the political sense. By providing a safe place, fresh air, and the benefits of limited but growing medical knowledge, these hospitals were in many ways progressive, their custodians doing their best in often difficult or impossible circumstances. But it would be wrong to ignore the realities: many regarded an outing to the original St Mary Bethlehem Hospital ('Bedlam') in London to view its unfortunates as a form of entertainment.

Sailing from Delirium: A pastiche of Yeats's *Sailing to Byzantium*.

Little Mal: A bowlie is a child's metal hoop; *Mochyn* – Welsh for a pig but applied to a grubby youngster — was used affectionately by my great aunts and grandparents to describe a mudlark, a tearaway. Abergavenny is the site of the former Pen-y-Fal Psychiatric Hospital.

Marion Morehouse: Ms Morehouse was the wife of the poet e.e.cummings; Florence Herman the wife of the poet William Carlos Williams, author of *The Red Wheelbarrow*.

Kempsey Murals: 'The Wests' were the notorious serial killers Fred and Rosemary West. They drove around Gloucestershire giving lifts to women, some of whom they murdered.

Kingfishers in Puzzle Wood: This is the reconstruction of a disorderly poem written by Charles William Edmondson, a cinema projectionist from Gloucestershire, who was admitted to the Bristol Asylum and diagnosed with Schizophrenia, Manic-Depressive Disorder, and Postural Disturbance. Although his condition was considered treatable, he died at the hospital eight years after his arrival. No other writings by him exist but he was known also to have been a talented painter. The references are to the Disney film *Snow White and the Seven Dwarfs* of 1937 and those employees of Walt Disney — Colvig, Harlan, La Verne, Costellati, Kahl, and Reitherman — who provided its voiced soundtrack. Puzzle Wood is an ancient woodland in the Forest of Dean showing evidence of Roman and possibly earlier open-cast mining. Its bizarre, moss-covered rock formations, with their sprouting ferns and trees, give it an other-worldly appearance.

Bodoni Bold: Giambattista Bodoni (1740-1813) was a designer of typefaces.

Alzheimer's Castle: Aricept, Exelon and Reminyl are drugs used to treat senile dementia; Lysandra is the Adonis Blue butterfly.

ACKNOWLEDGEMENTS

Some of these poems or earlier versions of them were published in magazines including *Agenda, Acumen, Poetry Wales, New Welsh Review, Poetry London, Poetry Ireland Review, Envoi, The Interpreter's House, Black Nore Review, Orbis, Staple, Lines Review, Lunar Poetry, Bangor Literary Journal* (Ireland), *The French Literary Review, Outposts, The Journal, Eclipse, Iota, PB* (Ireland), and *The English Chicago Review.*

I'm grateful to the volunteers at Glenside Museum, Fishponds, Bristol (formerly the Bristol Lunatic Asylum's church), for the custodial care with which they staff the building and look after its curios.

Cockatrice Books
Y diawl a'm llaw chwith

The cockatrice is hatched from a cockerel's egg, and resembles a dragon the size and shape of a cockerel. The English word is derived from the Latin *calcatrix*, but in Welsh it is called *ceiliog neidr*: 'adder-cock.' Its touch, breath and glance are lethal.

There is a saying in Welsh, *Y ddraig goch ddyry cychwyn*, which means, 'The red dragon leads the way.' The cockatrice spits at your beery patriotism.

www.cockatrice-books.com

FIVE GO TO SWITZERLAND
NIGEL JARRETT

A daughter curious about her widowed father's love life; a woman survivor of domestic abuse; a wife who learns something startling about her jazz-loving husband at his funeral; an old actor facing memory loss; a couple whose son was executed by militants; a black American academic staying in Wordsworth country while his university investigates a student complaint; an early 20th-century scullery maid being taught to read by a sinister manservant...

In his fourth wide-ranging and vivid short-story collection, award-winning writer Nigel Jarrett disturbs the unresolved tensions beneath the clear, slow-flowing waters of ordinary lives.

'Jarrett's stories take seemingly ordinary situations and tease out their complexity.'

Lesley McDowell, *The Independent*

'Vivid and vital stories that crackle like bushfire and ignite delight... I read them with unbridled pleasure and holy envy.'

Jon Gower

'Explaining what Jarrett does with language is a bit like trying to map gossamer with a chunky felt-tip.'

Mary-Ann Constantine

'A polymath of the written word... Every page has something to savour.'

Jonathan Lee, *Nation Cymru*

ANY KIND OF BROKEN MAN: COLLECTED STORIES
ROGER GRANELLI
with a foreword by Phil Rickman

A veteran of the war with Japan confronts the Japanese factory which has revivified his valley. An ageing Navajo on the edge of the desert meets his doctor son's white bride. A young jazz musician walks into a club with a pistol in his pocket, and a young criminal from the valleys who is suspected of murder finds peace of mind on a Scottish beach.

Grounded in the post-industrial communities of Wales, yet encompassing Spain, Malaysia and the Florida Keys, this collection spans the career of a prominent novelist from the early 1990s to the present day. Drug dealers, labourers, invalids and war criminals confront the start of a new century, the death of old certainties and old ways of life, the comforting weight of bitterness and the fearful beginnings beginnings of hope.

'Roger Granelli's books are incredibly hard to put down.'

The Big Issue

'From Emrys, the disillusioned old gentleman in the pub lounge who sleeps in a coffin, to the carer who owns the town's drug trade, or the gun-wielding jazz musician bored of bebop and seeking new thrills, Granelli paints his communities with respect and an understanding of the motivations behind every action, scandalous or mundane.'

Isabel Thomas, *Buzz*

RIVER OF HOPE
ROGER GRANELLI

For the doctor and missionary, Albert Schweitzer, life on the banks of the Ogowe river has settled into a kind of tranquillity. Since returning to Gabon from his wartime internment in France he has rebuilt his hospital, and when not treating his patients for leprosy, scabies or gangrene he has his music, his letters from his wife, and his books.

Then the Welshman, Adam Hope, comes to Lambaréné, a riverboat captain and trader in alcohol and timber, deeply troubled not only by his actions during the Great War but by his complicity in the injustices of colonialism. With him comes Pieters the Belgian, dissolute and degenerate, and between them they wield the power to destroy Schweitzer's work — or save it.

This new novel by the award-winning writer, Roger Granelli, is at once a vivid evocation of the beauties and horrors of the primeval forest, a profound meditation on redemption, violence and revenge; and an intricate portrayal of colonial relationships as Europe's age of dominance comes to an end.

'His characters breathe, make you care. One day the people that count will realise that Roger Granelli is... the best un-sung novelist in Wales.'

Phil Rickman

OF THE NINTH VERSE
A. L. REYNOLDS

Anwen and her younger brother, Idwal, are inseparable almost from birth. The childhood they share involves harvesting the hay and looking after the newborn lambs in the Conwy valley, though Anwen sees before her the promise of a degree in Edinburgh or Durham and a career as a mathematician, while Idwal seems destined by his strength and skill to take over the running of the family farm. Then, as Idwal's and Anwen's feelings for each other grow darker and more complex, she finds herself put to a terrifying choice.

With a luminous prose that reflects the richness of the Conwy Valley, A. L. Reynold's novel explores both the violent, destructive force of passion and the fragility of the human heart.

Of the Ninth Verse has a profound and rooted authenticity that convinces and enchants – an enthralling novel by a writer at the peak of her powers.'

Jim Perrin

a subtly-written, compelling narrative of forbidden yet irresistible love.

Angela Topping

For all its drama and sense of foreboding, *Of the Ninth Verse* is a strangely comforting read. And it is so much more than a novel about an illicit relationship. ...For me, it is the authenticity of the story that stays with you. *Of The Ninth Verse* is a love story. And a compassionate and incredibly convincing one at that.

Some Melodious Plot

SEASIDE TOWNS
A. L. REYNOLDS

For Anatoliy Yetvushenko, émigré and physicist, it should be the perfect holiday. Llandudno calls to his mind the Black Sea holidays of his childhood in Ukraine, while his companion, Francis, is just beginning to awaken to the possibilities of male sexual love in the first years following its legalisation. But Anatoliy has memories of an earlier holiday in Lyme Regis in the 1950s, where his previous lover, who now lives near Llandudno, left him to make a loveless marriage. With its awareness of the landscape of the north coast of Wales, of quantum physics and of deep time, this novel reflects the search for intimacy and fulfilment in the shadow of political tyranny and sexual persecution.

A chronicler of the region's disappearing heritage

North Wales Chronicle

'gentle yet searing, introspective yet intensely physical. A real gem of a book... Seek it out if you can.'

Rachel Rees, *Buzz*

'the wonder, the intensity, the profound gratitude of [sexual love]... the intimately human [cast] in an epic light, in the awesome interconnectedness of all'

Niall Griffiths, *Nation Cymru*

REASONING: TWENTY STORIES
ROB MIMPRISS

Reasoning is the first of three collections by Rob Mimpriss. It is followed by *For His Warriors* and *Prayer at the End.*

An old man tries to assess his guilt in the marriage his daughter has destroyed. A young man tries to understand why, in the same family, he should be both hated and loved. A seventeenth-century Puritan preacher and a Cardiff woman facing divorce unite in their call to 'know your innermost heart,' while a Romanian dissident under Ceaușescu and a Welsh-language activist find themselves outwardly liberated but inwardly still in chains.

'Through the stealthy movements of his prose, Rob Mimpriss enacts the quiet enigma of people's lives and relationships. The result is an understated fiction of compelling intensity.'

M Wynn Thomas

'Rob Mimpriss could be described as a quiet writer with a loud voice. It's good to know he's planning ahead. I'll be listening for more.'

Michael Nobbs, gwales.com

FOR HIS WARRIORS: THIRTY STORIES
ROB MIMPRISS

For His Warriors is the second of three collections by Rob Mimpriss. It is preceded by *Reasoning* and followed by *Prayer at the End.*

A Welsh farmer's wife during the Second World War kills the landgirl her husband has taken as his lover. A leader of the Cornish-language revival commits her last act of protest the day Russian troops march into Berlin. A lonely man on the waterfront in Llandudno wonders whether he or his girlfriend will be first to die of Aids, and a bored man in a restaurant in Cardiff Bay invents a story of arrest and torture to amuse his petulant lover.

'Both humour and pity often arise from the characters' inability to understand themselves and those close to them. In suggesting both the truth and the self-deception Mimpriss not only engages our sympathy but makes us question our assumptions about ourselves.'

Caroline Clark, gwales.com

PRAYER AT THE END: 23 STORIES
ROB MIMPRISS

Prayer at the End is the third of three collections by Rob Mimpriss. It is preceded by *Reasoning* and *For His Warriors*.

A cigarette quenched in the Menai Strait makes a man vow to live a selfish life. The memory of an unborn twin makes a man regret the selfish life he has lived. An elderly shopkeeper befriends the teenagers outside his shop, and a lonely householder sets out to confront the trespassers on his land.

'In the most seemingly unremarkable of Rob Mimpriss's pieces there is a skill, and a mystery and elusiveness to that skill, which other short-story writers might envy. This is a masterful collection.'

Gee Williams

'heaving with loss, regret and familial bonds.'

Annexe Magazine

PUGNACIOUS LITTLE TROLLS
ROB MIMPRISS

In his first three short-story collections, Rob Mimpriss painstakingly mapped the unregarded lives of Welsh small-town and country-dwellers. In Pugnacious Little Trolls, he combines the skill and quiet eloquence of his earlier work with confident experimentation, with stories set among the bird-bodied harpies of Central America, among the dog-headed Cynocephali of Central Asia, among humanity's remote descendants at the very end of the universe, and in the muddle of slag-heaps and job centres that H. G. Wells's Country of the Blind has become. In the three stories at the heart of the collection is Tanwen, idealistic and timid, embarking on her adult life in the shadow of global warming and English nationalism.

Where is the Welsh short story going? Wherever Rob Mimpriss takes it.
John O'Donoghue

bathed in white fire in every sense... Borges would happily own them.
Gee Williams

freely and fiercely inventive short stories... supercharged with ideas
Jon Gower, *Nation Cymru*

BV - #0082 - 241024 - C0 - 229/152/6 - PB - 9781912368464 - Matt Lamination